discovermore

Your Government

The Executive Branch

Ezra E. Knopp

Britannica Educational Publishing

IN ASSOCIATION WITH

Published in 2024 by Britannica Educational Publishing (a trademark of Encyclopædia Britannica, Inc.) in association with
The Rosen Publishing Group, Inc.
2544 Clinton Street, Buffalo, NY 14224

Distributed exclusively by Rosen Publishing.
To see additional Britannica Educational Publishing titles, go to rosenpublishing.com.

Editor: Caitie McAneney
Book Design: Rachel Rising

Photo Credits: Cover; (series background) Dai Yim/Shutterstock.com; Cover, Andrea Izzotti/Shutterstock.com; p. 4 Viktoriia Viktorovna/Shutterstock.com; p. 5 lev radin/Shutterstock.com; p. 6 https://commons.wikimedia.org/wiki/File:Allan_Ramsay_-_King_George_III_in_coronation_robes_-_Google_Art_Project.jpg: p. 7 Onur ERSIN/Shutterstock.com; p. 9 W. Scott McGill/Shutterstock.com; p. 9 Christopher Penler/Shutterstock.com; p. 10 Mark Van Scyoc/Shutterstock.com; p. 11 Miljan Mladenovic/Shutterstock.com; pp. 12, 17 Joseph Sohm/Shutterstock.com; p. 15 https://commons.wikimedia.org/wiki/File:Martin_Van_Buren_(colorized).jpg; p. 16 https://commons.wikimedia.org/wiki/File:President_Barack_Obama_with_full_cabinet_09-10-09.jpg#/media/File:President_Barack_Obama_with_full_cabinet_09-10-09.jpg; p. 19 https://commons.wikimedia.org/wiki/File:P20210526KR-0817_(51224817078).jpg; p. 19 Gerckens-Photo-Hamburg/Shutterstock.com; p. 20 Salma Bashir Motiwala/Shutterstock.com; p. 21 mark reinstein/Shutterstock.com; p. 22 White House Photography/Shutterstock.com; p. 23 Salma Bashir Motiwala/Shutterstock.com; p. 24 https://commons.wikimedia.org/wiki/File:Franklin_D._Roosevelt_-_NH_19.jpeg; p. 25 Salma Bashir Motiwala/Shutterstock.com; p. 26 Eliyahu Yosef Parypa/Shutterstock.com; p. 27 https://commons.wikimedia.org/wiki/File:Franklin_D._Roosevelt_in_Albany,_New_York_-_NARA_-_197241.jpg; p. 28 Salma Bashir Motiwala/Shutterstock.com; p. 29 Joseph Sohm/Shutterstock.com.

Cataloguing-in-Publication Data

Names: Knopp, Ezra E.
Title: The executive branch / Ezra E. Knopp.
Description: New York : Britannica Educational Publishing, in Association with Rosen Educational Services. 2024. | Series: Discover more: your government | Includes glossary and index.
Identifiers: ISBN 9781642828962 (library bound) | ISBN 9781642828955 (pbk) | ISBN 9781642828979 (ebook)
Subjects: LCSH: Executive departments--United States--Juvenile literature. | Presidents--United States--Juvenile literature. | Cabinet officers--United States--Juvenile literature.
Classification: LCC JK501.K66 2024 | DDC 351.73–dc23

Manufactured in the United States of America

Some of the images in this book illustrate individuals who are models. The depictions do not imply actual situations or events.

CPSIA Compliance Information: Batch #CSBRIT24. For further information contact Rosen Publishing at 1-800-237-9932.

Contents

Three Branches

The United States government is a **representative democracy** with an important job. The decisions of government officials impact everyone living in the nation. The government protects citizens against outside enemies and keeps order within the country. It provides services to its people and protects their rights.

Each branch's powers are given by the United States Constitution.

The head of the executive branch is the president. Joe Biden became president in 2021.

The U.S. government is made up of three parts, or branches. These are the executive branch, the legislative branch, and the judicial branch. The legislative branch makes laws. The judicial branch runs the courts and uses the Constitution and other laws to settle cases. The job of the executive branch is to carry out the laws. Let's learn more about the executive branch!

WORD WISE

A representative democracy is one in which leaders are chosen in elections. They are meant to represent the wishes of the people in the district that elected them.

We the People

The U.S. Constitution is the set of laws that the country was founded upon. After years of mistreatment by the British government, the Founding Fathers of the United States worked to create a constitution that made life fair for all citizens.

The newly independent citizens did not want an all-powerful ruler like British King George III, who they felt was a **tyrant**.

The Constitution starts with "We the People," showing that the country was supposed to work for all of its citizens.

In 1776, 13 colonies in North America declared independence from Great Britain. They fought a war for their independence and then formed the new country of the United States. The new nation's founders wrote the Constitution in 1787 to protect the rights of the country's citizens and ensure that one branch of government could not become more powerful than the others. In the United States, no one would be above the law—not even leaders.

WORD WISE

A tyrant is a ruler who has complete power over a country and who is cruel and unfair.

Keeping Each Branch in Check

To keep one branch from getting too powerful, the constitution makes sure each branch has some power to "check" the others. This is called a system of checks and balances. For example, the leader of the executive branch (the president) gets to appoint, or choose, many government leaders. But part of the legislative branch (the Senate) has the power to reject the president's choices.

Congress can charge the president with breaking the law. This charge is called impeachment. The Senate holds a trial to decide if the president is guilty. A guilty president must resign, or step down. The House of Representatives has impeached three presidents: Andrew Johnson, Bill Clinton, and Donald Trump. The Senate ruled all three not guilty, but impeachment is still a serious charge.

Senate hearings to approve or reject presidential choices for government leaders happen at the U.S. Capitol.

compareandcontrast

Each branch of the U.S. government has some power over the actions of the other two branches. Compare and contrast this system with one in which there are no checks and balances.

If a president is found guilty of impeachment charges, they cannot run for office again.

A President and Their Cabinet

The U.S. government's structure is set up in the Constitution. The executive branch is headed by the president of the United States. The president is joined in the executive branch by the vice president and a group of advisers called the cabinet. Each member of the cabinet is in charge of a separate department, such as the Department of Agriculture or Department of Education. Today there are 15 cabinet departments.

The Department of Transportation makes sure goods and people can travel around the country.

Cabinet members meet in the Cabinet Room of the White House.

Members of the cabinet must be approved by Congress. The president tries to choose men and women who have experience connected to their departments and who are likely to do a good job. The cabinet will meet regularly to talk about issues that are important to the nation.

Consider This

States also have an executive branch. The head of it is the governor. Who is the governor of your state?

Presidential Goals

Do you have a goal to be president someday? First, you need to know who can be president of the United States. The Constitution says that the president must be at least 35 years old, a natural-born U.S. citizen, and a resident of the United States for at least 14 years.

Barack Obama was elected as the first Black president in 2008, showing that people of minority groups could lead the country.

The first presidents were born British citizens, not American citizens. The first U.S.-born president was Martin Van Buren.

During the country's early years, only men who owned property could become president or even vote. This is no longer the case. Today, almost any American-born man or woman can become president. However, a person who has been proved guilty of a felony, or a very serious crime, cannot be president. People often vote for a person who has a vision for the nation that matches their own.

Consider This

Women and minorities didn't run for president for much of U.S. history. They were also kept from voting. How has this changed over time?

Electing a President

How do we choose the president of the United States? **Elections** are held to decide who will fill this important role. There are usually only two, sometimes three, serious candidates in an election. Most voters pick the candidate from the political party they most agree with. The Democratic Party and the Republican Party are the two major political parties in the United States.

A candidate can become president without winning the popular vote, or the most votes by citizens. This happened in 2016, when Donald Trump lost the popular vote to Hillary Clinton but won the electoral vote.

Political parties are groups of people who usually have similar beliefs about the role of government and how it should be run.

The president is not directly elected by individual voters. Instead, a group called the electoral college elects the president and the vice president. Electoral college members usually choose the candidate who won the popular vote in their state. Electoral votes are given to each state based on population. More populated states have more electoral votes.

WORD WISE

An election is the process of choosing someone for public office by voting.

What Does the Vice President Do?

A presidential candidate chooses a vice presidential candidate to run with them in an election. A lot of thought goes into picking the right candidate for vice president. If the president dies or resigns, the vice president becomes president. The vice president has to be prepared to lead the nation.

Joe Biden was Barack Obama's vice president before becoming the president of the United States.

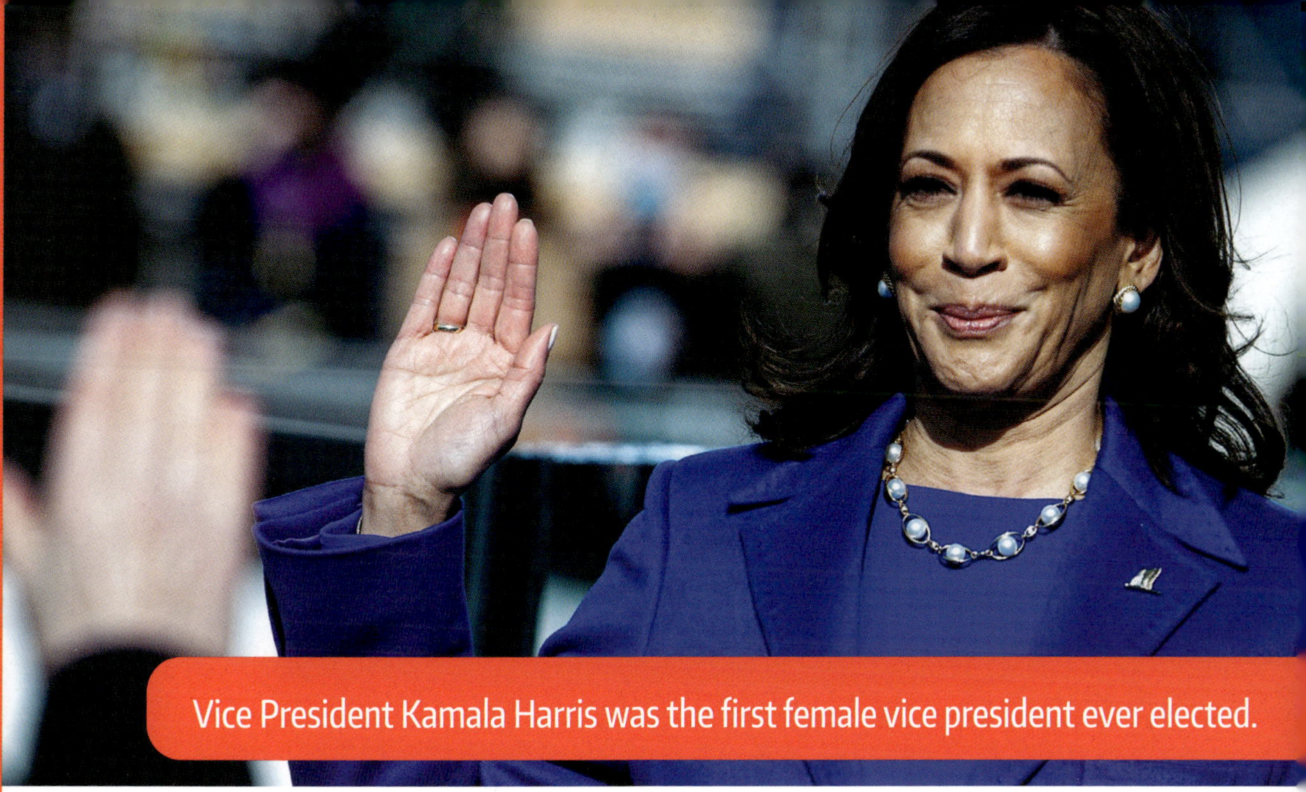

Vice President Kamala Harris was the first female vice president ever elected.

The vice president's only real duty is to serve as the president of the Senate. If a Senate vote is tied, the vice president casts the deciding vote. The vice president also leads cabinet meetings if the president is away. Vice presidents do a lot of work with members of Congress to get laws passed and to support the president. Sometimes, vice presidents run for president later on.

Why might a former vice president make a good president?

Help and Advice

Presidents have a lot of important decisions to make that can affect the country, and even other countries. That's why they have a staff that can offer help and advice, led by the chief of staff. The agencies, or departments, in the executive office handle many day-to-day tasks that the president is too busy to take on. These agencies include the Office of Management and Budget and the National Security Council.

The White House Office is also part of the executive office. It is made up of the president's personal staff members. This includes advisers, experts, and people who help the president communicate with Congress and the press. For example, the White House press secretary answers questions from the press and gives them information.

Some White House staff members travel with the president on Air Force One.

compare and contrast

The members of the cabinet often focus on big-picture topics. Workers in the executive office usually work out the details of their ideas. Why are both roles important?

Karine Jean-Pierre became the first Black White House press secretary in 2022.

Veto Power

Some people think the president can make laws, but that's not true. Only the legislature (Congress), can do that. For a law to be made, a member of Congress has to introduce it as a document called a bill. The president works with the White House Office and the cabinet to make suggestions about the bill. The bill is then crafted by Congress. The two houses of Congress must agree on the bill and vote on it. If the bill is approved, it goes to the president.

The veto is one of the president's most powerful tools for shaping laws.

A president can veto any bill. Here, former president Ronald Reagan signs a veto message.

The president then must decide either to sign the bill or to **veto**, or block, it. Once it is signed, it becomes law. If it is vetoed, Congress will have to fix the bill or write a new one.

WORD WISE

The veto is a power described in the Constitution that allows the president to block bills and other official acts before they become law.

Presidential Powers

The president has two kinds of powers granted by the Constitution: enumerated powers and implied powers. Enumerated powers are those that are mentioned directly in the Constitution. They give the president the power to carry out certain duties. These are the powers to veto bills, pardon prisoners, carry out federal laws, and command the nation's military. Enumerated powers also include appointing people to important posts and justices to the Supreme Court.

The president often chooses justices who share their values. President Joe Biden chose Ketanji Brown Jackson to serve on the U.S. Supreme Court.

The president can also meet with representatives from other nations and make **treaties**.

Appointing Supreme Court justices is a lot like appointing cabinet members. The president wants qualified candidates who will do a good job and who can be approved by Congress. The Supreme Court is the highest court in the country so this is a very important job.

WORD WISE

Treaties are official agreements that are made between two countries or groups.

The other kind of powers given to the president are implied powers. These ones aren't clearly written in the constitution. Instead, the wording of the document suggests that they are available to the president. Implied means to express something in an indirect way. Implied powers include organizing the executive branch, making executive orders, and beginning military action.

Some presidents have made only a few executive orders. Others have issued thousands. Franklin D. Roosevelt issued the most of any president.

Joe Biden signed more than a dozen executive orders on his first day as president.

Executive orders are statements by the president that must be obeyed like laws. Presidents can use executive orders to make important decisions without consulting with Congress. Presidents also sometimes issue executive orders to change the way earlier bills are enforced, or made effective. However, Congress may overturn an executive order with a new law or refuse to fund it.

Consider This

In 1970, President Richard Nixon issued an executive order to establish the Environmental Protection Agency to protect the health of people and the environment. How was this executive order beneficial to the nation?

Four Years

A president can't stay in office forever. There's a limit on the number of years they can have this job. Presidents serve four-year stretches of time called terms. After the first four years, the president can run again or step aside for another candidate to run. Most presidents who complete their first term choose to run again.

A president who runs again and wins is reelected and serves a new term. This is the second inauguration, or admission into office, of Barack Obama in 2013.

Franklin D. Roosevelt was president from 1932 to 1945.

Presidents can be elected to only two terms. This was not always the case, and several presidents have run for more terms. Only Franklin D. Roosevelt was ever elected to more than two terms. He was elected to four terms. Term limits ensure that a person does not become president for life or gain unfair power.

Consider This

The 22nd Amendment to the Constitution limits presidents to two terms of office. Why would lawmakers think this limit was important?

A New President

What happens when a president's last term is over? Then, it's time for the president-elect, or the person who was just elected for the role, to take office. In the United States, it is common to have a peaceful transfer of power. The president who is leaving often gives advice to the president-elect.

The president-elect officially becomes president in a ceremony called the **inauguration** that takes place on January 20.

At the inauguration, the president-elect takes the oath of office from the chief justice of the Supreme Court.

In this photograph, four former U.S. presidents walk together, even though they had different views and ideas while in office.

In most cases, the new president hires an entirely new staff of advisers. Cabinet members are usually replaced with people who share the new president's values. It's up to the new president and vice president to build relationships in Congress to get work done. They have only a few years to make a positive impact on the American people.

WORD WISDOM

An inauguration is an event that introduces someone into a job or position with a formal ceremony.

Glossary

advisers: People who give an opinion or suggestion to someone about what should be done.

appoint: To choose someone for a particular job or to give someone a position or duty.

cabinet: A group of people who give advice to the leader of a government.

chief of staff: A person of high rank who advises a leader (such as the U.S. president) on important matters.

citizens: People who legally belong to a country and have the rights and protection of that country.

constitution: A system of beliefs and laws by which a country or state is governed.

document: An official paper that gives information about something or that is used as proof of something.

issue: To give something to someone in an official way, or to announce something in a public or official way.

judicial branch: The part of government that uses the U.S. Constitution and other laws of the U.S. government to settle legal cases.

legislative branch: The part of government that has the power to make laws.

military: Relating to soldiers or the armed forces (such as the army, navy, marines, and air force).

minority: A group of people who are different from the larger group in a country or other area in some way, such as race or religion.

pardon: To officially say that someone who is guilty of a crime will be allowed to go free and will not be punished.

qualified: Having the necessary skill, experience, or knowledge to do a particular job or activity.

role: A part played by a person or thing.

security: The state of being protected or safe from harm.

For More Information

Books

Chang, Kirsten. *President*. Minneapolis, MN: Bellwether Media, 2021.

Rose, Rachel. *President Joe Biden: America's 46th President.* Minneapolis, MN: Bearport Publishing, 2021.

Stratton, Connor. *President.* Lake Elmo, MN: Focus Readers, 2024.

Websites

Executive Branch: The President

www.ducksters.com/history/us_executive_branch.php

Learn more about what the president does as the leader of the executive branch.

Presidential Fun Facts

kids.nationalgeographic.com/history/article/presidential-fun-facts

Explore fun facts about past presidents, such as George Washington and Franklin Delano Roosevelt.

Index